Paradise Reflections

Mary Schneider

BookLeaf Publishing

Presentation by *BookLeaf Publishing*

Web: www.bookleafpub.com

E-mail: info@bookleafpub.com

ISBN: 9789357442862

First edition 2023

For my parents, who taught me to dream.

For Ed, whose belief in me led me to believe in myself, and encouraged me to make my dreams come true.

Up Up and Away

a rumble

just to start

frantic beating
of my heart

speed increasing
fast
and faster
and even faster
shaking wings and then up

climbing higher with the world askew
everything familiar is small and smaller and then

Gone

Gliding

Soaring

Floating

at Forty Thousand Feet

Dream Maker

Dreams come true
through hoping
and scheming
and careful detail

With research
and planning;
Strong will and
persistence prevail

It may not seem easy,
it's not, this is true.
But the one to rely on,
my Darling, is you.

There is no one to stop you,
nay, none but yourself
Keep track of your dreams
And invest in your health.

It's worth it, I promise
Your every last dream
And I know that sometimes
Too hard, it will seem

Don't rely upon others
to make dreams come true
The dream maker, my Darling?
The dream maker is you.

Choices

I walked upon the beach one day
Not knowing what I'd find,
And scattered all along the way
were tiny bits of shine

I paid them no attention,
Spoke to a friendly guy
He was so kind to share with me
Where turtles did reside

Upon the reef, not far from shore
He found a turtle nest
I thought about my snorkel and
I really thought it best

To go and get it from the room
So I too could enjoy
The sight of turtles resting
beyond the bobbing buoy

I stepped back from the water
and received a gentle push
A friendly woman stopped me
To show me jellyfish

Scattered all along the beach
She smiled and gave me warning
she did not want me to get stung
on this delightful morning

I thanked her for her kindness,
And turned to share the news
But the turtle man was far away
Enjoying turtle views.

I had no way to reach him
I could not let him know
I hoped a sting would not disrupt
his morning turtle show

I stood there on the beach
and I wondered what to do
Do I ignore the danger
to enjoy the turtle view?

I would not see the jellyfish
if I were in the sea
For safety's sake then, on the beach
Was where I ought to be

And yet, as I looked out to sea
my eyes turned toward the reef,
Her warning didn't seem so kind
It just felt like a thief.

Whipped Cream Wisdom

Three little girls dressed for the beach
With mom standing on the boardwalk
Morning joggers fly by
Some go fast
Some go slow
Three little cups filled with whipped cream
Savored as mom drinks her morning latte
The tallest girl examines the palm trees
As the morning light filters through
The middle girl watches the pigeons
As they fight over a discarded muffin
The youngest peers over her coffee cup
At the joggers as they fly by
"Mommy, why are they running?"
Mom is still searching for the second adult
Explains it's a sidewalk, where people often run.
Reaches for her phone, ends the conversation.
Consideration.
A pout turns to a frown
A whisper, so low no one else can hear:
"But why are they RUNNING
it's VACATION and they're DOING it
WRONG"

Steadfast Majesty

The clouds surround the mountains
Cloaking them with mystery
Shrouding them in silence
Keeping the secrets of the summits
Providing protection for their peaks

Or do the mountains stretch to reach them?
Perhaps the clouds bring comfort allowing them
to
Hide from horrors they've lived long enough to
see
Enduring in their existence such history
I can only gaze upon their greatness

Moonset

The night is calm
Silent
The moon dances through the stars
As they make their nightly trek
Across the sky

Ever changing
Even the sea
Pays attention to the moon
Using her guidance to bring
the King waves

Reflecting
Providing light as day-dwellers
End their days
And night-dwellers
begin theirs.

Silently streaking across the sky
No production, not seeking attention.
Simple reflection
Yet pulls the eye.

She enters slowly,
After the sun's dramatic exit
And enlongated goodbye.
She makes sure to not appear
Before he has gone

And yet
She leaves the same way
As the sun makes his presence known
with blinding light and trumpet blare
She watches the show
And slowly

silently

slips

away

The Sea

building, swelling, rolling, crashing
waves come from the sea
swimming, playing, racing, laughing
dolphins in the sea
surfing, snorkeling, photographing
humans in the sea

the sea can never be denied
the sea can never try to hide
its presence noticed everywhere
surrounds the land and salts the air
providing food, creating mood
with storms or balmy breeze

Heartsong

Palm trees sway in the island breeze
Whales sing their glorious song
waves dance upon the sand
to sweep back and come back again
Blue skies and the mountains high
Rainbows gleam from daily rain
Hawaii sings a beautiful song
only the heart can hear

Hawaiian Sunrise

Breaking through the morning haze
One by one, I see the rays
They glow and beam so very bright
Bringing joy and such delight

Orange and yellow, firey red
Who could ever stay in bed
and miss the painted morning sky,
A work of art made for the eye?

The sea reflects the colors bright
A crowd has gathered with delight.
Together we watch, together we sigh
Another Hawaiian sunrise gone by.

Neverending

crashing on the sand
swelling, building, on the rise
just to crash again

Pacific Pace

Endless summer, endless sun-
endless ways to have some fun.

Daily rainbows, forever a breeze-
no such thing as humidity.

Tropical flowers aplenty
wave in the air, oh so gently.

Palm-lined paths with friendly faces-
smiling people and beautiful places.

Water glistening in the sun with
Stunning sunset when day is done

The Tourist

Turquoise water
Sky azure
Cotton clouds
and sandy shore

Lucious fruits and
Fragrant brews-
Taste the islands
There's much to choose

Flowered shirts
And jewelry too
A piece of paradise
Goes home with you

The Wedding

A light in the eyes
A song in the heart
to come together
and never to part

Excitement and nerves
a sprinkle of stress
His tux and his shoes
Her hair and her dress

Food, music, flowers
It all has to be planned
sometimes it's a DJ
sometimes it's a band

Her family, his family
Traditions collide
The crowd gathers and waits
And then it is time

So many decisions
to create just one day
But the crucial part
is the promise they'll say

The Promise

A vow from the heart
a promise for life
'til death do us part
as husband and wife

To honor and cherish
through sickness and health
through debt and through poverty
(but hopefully, wealth)

Three little words
are often enough
to be spoken and heard
and confess one's true love

Today love is spoken
with not three words, but two
To look at each other
and promise "I do"

Diamondhead

Ancient Sentinel
Watching o'er the sandy shore
Caught in every shot
Created in one moment
Never to be forgotten

Hawaiian Dream

I dreamed of paradise
and wondered what I'd find
No matter what I did
'twas always back of mind

A lifelong dream I harbored
to finally go one day
Serenity I found there
'tis more than I can say

The days were all so happy
no sorrow to be found
Pacific breeze upon my face
my feet on island ground

The memories will hold me
And through my life I'll go
Until at last, I travel back
Again we'll meet, I know

Quiet Mornings

Fire licks the early air
from torches scattered 'round
Island music everywhere
From hidden speakers on the grounds

Peaceful breeze and muted waves
Cobblestones lead to the sand
Rustling leaves on wavy palms
Steaming coffee in my hand

The ocean tumbles out in front
The palm trees stand behind
And farther back, the lovely grounds
Are pond- and flower-lined

Morning fun has not begun
The beach is empty still
The joggers stretch before they run
And I just look my fill

Paradise Views

Palm Trees gently sway
wispy Clouds roll overhead
in the deep blue skies
Ocean glistens in the sun
Views so sweet in Paradise

www.ingramcontent.com/pod-product-compliance
Lightning Source LLC
Chambersburg PA
CBHW051721130826
49812CB00034B/1295
* 9 7 8 9 3 5 7 4 4 2 8 6 2 *